ASTERISKS

DAVID WEVILL

Toronto

Exile Editions

2007

OVER 30 YEARS OF PUBLISHING

Library and Archives Canada Cataloguing in Publication

Wevill, David, 1935-
    Asterisks / David Wevill.

Poems.

ISBN 978-1-55096-095-2
    I. Title.

PS8545.E85A78 2007   C811'.54   C2007-901444-5

Cover photograph *Sunrise off the coast of Turkey* by Michael Callaghan

Design and Composition by Homunculus ReproSet
Typeset in Birka and Georgia at the Moons of Jupiter Studios
Printed in Canada by Gauvin Imprimerie

The publisher would like to acknowledge the financial assistance of
the Canada Council for the Arts and the Ontario Arts Council.

First published in Canada in 2007 by Exile Editions Ltd.
144483 Southgate Road 14
General Delivery
Holstein, Ontario, N0G 2A0
info@exileeditions.com
www.ExileEditions.com

Canadian Sales & Distribution: U.S. Sales & Distribution:
McArthur & Company   Independent Publishers Group
c/o Harper Collins   814 North Franklin Street
1995 Markham Road   Chicago, IL 60610
Toronto, ON M1B 5M8   www.ipgbook.com
toll free: 1 800 387 0117   toll free: 1 800 888 4741

For Guit, who is here.

To row through the silence
THOMAS TRANSTROMER

The most beautiful is the object
which does not exist
ZBIGNIEW HERBERT

*

1.

Shredded pulp, glue
of history,
          page upon page
pressed flat. In every word
in and between each cry

a body, a some
one, not
clothed or naked or named

Let the sun
attend to this,
fingers of concrete
feet spared the grass

Cut us doors less tall
so we may enter on our knees

Look down Look down.

*

2.

They're digging the field
that took them in
from exile in the sand

The man bent double can see
where a woman
lay down with her child

Ant, she sings
come home
to where
distress has no other smell

now, ever.

*

3.

Two branches
Two birds
   one eating
   one watching

if one were to fly off
the other would have no purpose

More to
where you are
than
here I am.

*

4.

Legs legs
little girl springs
    up and down
apart from where
the wind goes, a part

of the wind
who is a junkie with a clear head
a capsized star
in its youngest sex

Has her own name
jumps higher and higher
to reach to touch it.

*

5.

The lifesnake uncoils
into that hole
where water
is driest   On a billboard

a woman is swimming
away, toward sunset
    and life returns
        where you were

rain silences by touch
the apple of thought.

*

6.

When the blade falls
between seasons too slow to notice
or fear and happiness
    tongue in a dry mouth
avid to taste again

All images spent
in the long search for one
    that needs nothing more
than a brave sunset on a blue sea

to settle upon like a white bird
at rest on the endlessness of an expanding wave

no street address
the same
as any other.

*

7.

Is there life after
poetry?   All that the
past caught would
perhaps,
return to itself—
          mind gone back
now, to life's proper calling,
life.

Some things will dance
and others will lie still.

If we detect a singing
it is theirs.

*

8.

quick strokes of the pen
marking time. Not sounds
but shapes for sounds

Where can I hide
asked the child

By noon
windabsent. Clouds
wet or dry, climb
        hand over hand
the day's heat

Where, asked the child
is my selfshape, place to hide

a sound
within a sound

a breathing in, not out.

*

9.

This mark refers you to
another place
      fire, her star
an unpronounceable name
whose wherebeing
      kept old light

She had a way with her
What lovers saw
      or missed
in her eyes
was an ancient event
a murdered light
      gone black

Texture of an empty chair

vacated air.

*

10.

Winter makes better poems
better moons

Name
no mere name
no name
        merely name

quanta, light
up there
where things fall

Sing
birds of dawn

the unidentifiable
that is always there

Light
pitting a tin roof
like rain.

*

11.

Dreams: radical doors
forever open, closed

Wake at night to the crying of a spotted fawn
taken by something—

unknown yet familiar
city of strangers
all on first-name terms
          whose meanings are forbidden

Here there has been a death
or a vanishment—
self, cold-case detective
in search of his shadow

          too late, as often
among the clueless footprints
leading here or there

choose whichever.

*

12.

We come home in the sense
there is that,
waiting or gone.

A deep
vowel draws us. Otherwise
what lurks in pastures
or lingers in dark city streets

is air that touches
nothing.

An old sandal
its mate lost
is home. The air
in an emptied pen.

Not examples, images.

Memory of a loving hand
stroking
what night
makes afraid.

*

13.

Spotted fawn is back.
Then what was that cry the other night?

No, there were three.
Lucky or unlucky three.

Both eyes
and the eye between,
the hidden bead of wisdom.

Sincerity of milk.

Duck between mother's legs
and life will flow.

Deer crowd the little lawn.
Rush-hour as I scatter food.

One hand, a dozen mouths.
The furred air we breathe.

*

14.

True form
   of no-form

It is after and before
memory

I separate
water from water
    with my hands

What is there
was predictable, but
who would have guessed
    it is this

air the live-oak fills.

*

15.

Every poem, however
obscure, is a revealment

Before this
there was nothing

Air
costs so much,
breath, lives

The desert's dead children
continue to grow,
grow beyond the lives
they might have uttered

Silence though is heroic
Silence is
the future that precedes

breath.

*

16.

When a man and woman
separate
the children follow
where they can—

The wind outside the door
open its arms,
and what was a breath across
face, hair

becomes a body
without a name
with open arms.

No one leaves entirely.

Look around you and see
which side your shadow falls—

Spin round, spin round
to catch it as it falls.

*

17.

They scattered the fires
and rode on.
A few bones
catch the wind and drift off as ash.

What talk costs...

In the future are settlements.
Now
dusty soldiers go elsewhere
and breed new freedoms.

Have a good day.

We in turn
sleep less
and make it count.

*

18.

What have you done to yourself?

The fruits you loved to eat
        peel and eat
slice gently open to make
        perfect tongue-tip bites

in season
each in season—
everything and everyone
in season—

Life always replenished itself
always
        fruits in season—

Until

no pit
    no seed
        no stone

your hands went empty.

*

19.

The knife-cut knuckle
almost hides its scar,
        my singular addiction
to old wounds.

In the village street
a drunk fell
and crawled away
up steepness into darkness.

Dry summer, dry year.

Then that night, a sprinkle
"Rain", spat José,
"I call that bird-piss".

The pictures faded now.

Old olive sacks
the memories
ripped and tossed aside.

*

20.

After so long heat
mindbone picked clean

Burnt in the light
between halves—

    one eye
    another eye

Is the rain
    fire's enemy
merciful to fire

or does the occasion matter
the time of mind
    between darknesses

To love
To be of use.

*

21.

Tu Fu: "How will poems
bring honor?"

I cut at this—
So that we talk about—

beauty of
fine language.

The soldiers of dust
want to come home now.
Blood mixed with dust

is metaphor.

As dying is like
nothing.
          Help me ask

a question that has no answer.
A poem nothing can read

but itself.

*

22.

Light, colorless
as numbers are colorless
as memory
                loses
vividness

As memory aquires grief
and grief's opposite
        grieflessness
wit in the playing down of things

In the dry leaves
a child falls dead
gets up again
                gets up
and the game goes on
against the play of bare walls

Lights off   Lights on
the sun unlocks its world

The sun
remembers to.

*

23.

October, the hands spread
then fall away

At the mind's edge
distant sound of bombing
              only the wind,
·deafening light.

Clarity of skies above history
in a child's picturebook—

Who talks to begin a sentence
end a thought
              before words
turn cold—

Soul of a sparrow
pecks at bread
beneath a café table—

It's time to go, move on
as you said once, and did.

*

24.

Village, hills, blue sea

You look for something
that isn't there,
so you invent the thing
you're looking for—

Wheat, olives, vines, figs
the plains for progress
the hills for mere survival

Same crop at different altitudes,
different harvest months
but the same prayers—

Earth, heart,
opens so very slowly

rain, wind, sun
and the swallows come and gone
each one nameless.

*

25.

There comes a point
where large and small
    are identical—

an eye
and everything it sees
    encompassed in one glance—

Some line is now being crossed
that stays in place
    until it is time again

to resume, retrace
if only, now, as a shadow
    the lengthening spiral of words

that ancient path between fields

that brought us here.

*

26.

Twitchtail squirrel
headdown down the tree
for water, comes—

quick neighbor of mine
eats, drinks, at the cat's bowl
when the cat's not there

Drought all winter now
fires across the high plains
     the rain is angry
New Year's come and gone

Another stick from my fire
waits to light itself
with whatever breath I save

Old man Old wind

squirreltails.

*

27.

One by one they go
    the old languages
        the little tongues

Birdwings heard at daybreak
they enter and leave
the back way—

There there
old ones
    old songs
        old bones of songs.

*

28.

Syllables, buried like nuts
at half-forgotten points
in the strawdry winter grass.

What don't wake
don't sleep.

Once or twice
in an old love letter
the words come back, to say
close to a one that spoke once

where have you gone.

*

29.

Sunburst, August '45
city gone
     wasted eyes

through the fire
darkly gone. To hide
is to be forever at large—

burned on memory
     on white stone
eyes that crowd my darkness—

Eyes who lived
who found the sun

Nothing, nothing to be done.

*

30.

Grass inflames the sky
Grass and the inarticulate gifts of grass
go up, up.

Smoke is a verb.
Wind is a verb.
Grass is a noun, like stone.

Words burn away words.

Set a dish of poetry under a tree.
A bird will find it, some creature.

Oh, it cries.
what now what now.

*

31.

The old painter
took the color ochre
scraped away at the mountain
to the mountain's bones

Under the hot dry sun
the broad hat
    his fierce eye thinking

In the past tense so much is
possible.
        Old men should
learn to shut up.

There are other ways to be
than talk about it.

Waste is not good.
Waste is never kindly.

*

32.

I am not carried away
by poetry.

If a poem were to
carry me off, I'd say

put me down, we've
come a long way together.

Now tell me
what it was all about.

Oh, nothing. Nothing.

*

33.

If it is the nature of women
to scream, and men to shout
the rest, by right, is silence.

Snow drifting over our
forgiven names
whiting that human darkness.

I love the evening sunlight
north of the house. Her voice
from the kitchen calling me, come help.

Heaven is dry of blood. Air
fills the veins of the saved
whispering, mercy, mercy on us.

Such little breaths
from which the rain comes.

*

34.

the lovely irrecapturable
details. Dendrites
of snow adrift on air, becalmed
          like a leaf in ice.

Oktoberfest
          Boppard-am-Rhein '62
the innkeeper's wife said
          We do not take Jews here
(meant, but didn't say it)

Mutterland
          Vaterland
Arminius did for Varus
          in the Teutoburger Wald 9 A.D.
Panzers through winterforest in '44
          Your eyes
                    Your hair
                              Shulamit.

Downriver then
to hunt for shelter and food.

Down river, unforgiven
till love do us part.

*

35.

When a poem goes for a walk
it whistles up the neighbor's dog,
it breathes a thousand smells.

Tree, who are you
to tell me I'm not one.

Smoke over the river

Sun gone down.

*

36.

A hand raised
in greeting, or
to ward off the sun.

That, I say
is my brother. Walks

with the slow gait of a horse
or wind through the tall fieldgrass

across forty seven years

pencilmarks
by the kitchen door

lengths of children
his years so much less.

*

37.

You came back that time
torn, a pale transparency

a fragment of life, light
a nuance, barely

Time steps across your eyes now
a pattern of mounting numbers
many as rain

You are ungathered history
Your name waits, waits
to be fingered, spoken.

Voice in a thimble, bone
sing me again
that reckless wild green song.

*

38.

First day of spring, I tell the grass.
Grass has the nerve
      to come back green.

Old discarded work-glove
full of gesture—
      not wind, not hand.

Owl takes flight at twilight.

Transtromer:
      to row through
           the silence.

Syntax burns off as it speaks.

Poetry   the far nearness of rain.

*

39.

Not an elegant war
this, as wars go. Spilt
blood smells ugly
  even onscreen.

The combed administrative suits
keep open mouths. They
mumble, for silence has
  an ugly sound.

Spilt, not over grass
or in dust, the blood, but
on cracked pavement
  that doesn't drink

but dries death up. Nothing
but the sun has
such thirst. Not even
  right and wrong.

*

40.

Song—

as the wind rose
they talked just briefly

Are we responsible for
what we say.
                    If so
why speak.

And the rain fell
and couldn't get up again.

Come to me now, he said.
I'm but a plain chest of drawers
built by a clumsy carpenter.

Song—
as the rain fell.

*

41.

Let a voice go and it
may run and hide.

Dry tears
of a lizard on a stone.

A poem, say, tragically in love
with a poem it has never met,

one that could release it
from the terrifying obligation to speak—

Together they might breed
new silences. Smell

water in the desert.
Wake with that hope.

*

42.

It is a gift, this
green quiet of uncertainty
between words—

fertile speechlessness.

After before falls
the whole of time before
after recurs—
        a mask thrown high in the wind

lands where, or cannot
anywhere.
            A child
begins her song, and then forgets—

Such wide eyes of forgetting!

Who can think
this is not a loss

but a prize.

*

43.

A poem brought to light
returns to its darkness.
The remainder is words.

Grown old, you become
what you reach for,
can touch, without breaking.

Take beauty and
divide it into lines—
flute notes, a warbler's song

rises
      curves
            falls
scatters like rain off a tree.

Beauty is indivisible. The
remainder's an echo of light
in keeping with words.

*

44.

Here, there, memory fails
made up by threads of fiction.
Something must fill the holes

the spaces, the silence
so the fabric holds.

You are now my creation
as I am in part yours.
Stupidity, happiness, pain

we are one landscape,
where the light was once at home
but moved, has moved on—

wind above the mind, running, walking
the quick bodiless presence.

You, said the old one, and you,
join hands now. Be careful.

*

45.

Subject to object: sun wind rain
joined in ways language has
no hands for.

Words precede the unborn life—
hopes, fears, a name.

The homeless poem
grazes alone in some neighbor's field.
Lightyears are its substance.

It leaves no evidence
it was ever alive.

No soft prints in the snow.
No feather falls from the sky.

I am open
says the door.

*

46.

The moon's phallic track across the water.
Munch's dispossessed lovers.
Summer's northern silence.

Not that things come and go
but are always there. One
earth, one century—

late or soon. The details multiply
that tell time. The opening
and closing of a hand. Two hands.

Once we had a house on a northern river.
Others now, no names left of that time.

Lovers dispossessed
become poems. That other silence.

*

47.

The word fingers contains
the word griefs
            the n left over
wanders

join hands now.

Over whose body are you likely
to pray
            as a tree its shadow

knowing that, and that
                        alone
is every season you own—

there—

breathtakingly—

*

48.

Say repetition is really
a recollecting forward

mutant cancer gene
in the family's blood

I thought I drank with the sun
but it was the moon, all along

the moon's
lovely long blood vowel

At the tomb of the unknown poem
they gather, intoning an ancient song

Orpheus Orpheus

The words won't come.

*

49.

Not to
say something, but
to say
toward something, I think

says it.

In an hour the sun will rise.
There are no clouds.

Watch with me.

ACKNOWLEDGEMENTS

Nos. 1-7 appeared in *Borderlands*, Texas Poetry Review, No. 25, and in Spanish translation in *Turia*, Revista Cultural, No 75, Teruel, Spain.

Nos. 8-10 appeared in *Future Welcome, The Moosehead Anthology X* (edited Todd Swift).

Nos. 11-21 appeared in *Exile The Literary Quarterly*, Vol. 30, No. 1.

I wish to thank these publications and their editors.